A Spark of Soul

Melanie McCurdie

Copyright © 2018 Melanie McCurdie
All rights reserved.
ISBN-13: 978-1717277404
ISBN-10: 1717277403

Dedication

le langage humain n'a pas de mot pour
exprimer les profondeurs de mon cœur

For infinity and longer

A Spark of Soul

Acknowledgement

As always, for Muse

For my bestest bestie
I miss you and I love you.

For my sisters and brothers by heart,
thank you.

Greetings adventurer! Before you begin, a few discretionary words:

Everything written from this point forward is to be considered snippets from my own twisted imagination and/or my own opinion.

The words that follow are not an official representation of any human, animal (warm blooded or cold blooded), extradimensional beings and/or biologically challenged individuals.

Actual offences, feelings or emotions may vary from individual to individual. If conditions persist, stop reading. Some reassembly may be required. Batteries and weapons not included. Objects in mirror *are* closer than they appear.

My gratitude does not include tax, title, license or freedom from further subjection to bloodsauce.

Enjoy your read.

M xo

My Son

He talked
About everything
To everybody
Then two years ago
He said words
but stopped talking
I watched him grow
Watched him grow his mind
Now I realise that
its the quality in the words
He chooses to share.

Friday Night

I'm sitting here
In the dark
With my head
Under the covers
And toes exposed
Watching a movie
With the earbuds in
The kind where everybody screams
Eating cheese like a weirdo
And I can't help thinking
That it'd be more fun with company

Melanie McCurdie

Timpani Drums

If you have never grieved,
If you have never denied
the finality of reality
If you have never felt the
Timpani drums of your heart
Pounding and screaming in your ears
NO NO NO NO NO NO NO NO
and felt the weight of Reaper's
sad, lonely gaze on your soul
Then you have no business
telling somebody else
how to mourn

It's a good question

I just don't understand.
I can't comprehend
how using actual words
does not make you heard.
Then WHY, exactly
am I wasting my breath
talking to a deaf world
full of people singing
🎤 me me me 🎤 ?
I suppose ...
I like the sound of my own voice?
Still, it's a good question

Melanie McCurdie

Neither bats nor bears

I truly think that
the community of man,
is not meant to be
awake so much
We aren't nocturnal
Not by nature or design
We are not bats nor bears,
so we don't hibernate.
Except by choice or through
a divine act; call it a
interjection of benevolence
from some derelict deity

bubbles

Sometimes, when i'm alone/
almost by myself cos ghosts/
i wear pink with no makeup/
and let my hair go curly/
and pretend that i'm a warm/
blooded, a soft hearted girl/
instead of the cold minded/
all but invisible weirdo/
laying shrouded in bubbles/
adding salt to the water/
that is the truer image/
floating on the razors edge.

Melanie McCurdie

Shell

All that you see is a hard shell
The veneer is a result of my time,
Trapped in the Hellmouth's yaw
It's like rock, baby, unbreakable
Maybe you think I'm some snarcastic schnook
With an IDGAF attitude and a
sarcastic left hook; you're not wrong
Hey, I'm strong but smell ain't everything,
not made of stone or steel or
even spit and goodwill most days.
Duct tape is a staple around here
Truth is, inside is just a tired human
who needs a soft quiet place to break
and resemble the pieces of my jigsaw heart
I'll still destroy you if you push me though ...

burden

Lately I feel like I've become a burden
No matter how often I get told
I hear people talking and still -
I'm not that difficult to be around
self centred enough to want to
talk about me for a change
maybe how my day was or how's the weather

I feel like I've been thrown aside
without so many words spoken
I don't do hints, not well,
but it sure sounded that way and I'm sad

Melanie McCurdie

Wanna be Hoth

I went outside again today
It was very bright and loud
There was fucking snow everywhere but
The sun was all sunny
MAKE UP YOUR MIND!!
All this as the doors to that
Wanna be Hoth out there
Come closer and closer
It caused my chest to freeze up
And I started to sweat
Because I wore no makeup
Because I forgot I needed to
But I stepped out anyway
Screamed for effect
But it didn't kill me
It might seem weird to be excited but
I went outside again today
I knew hell was cold ...

Psyche Soother

I am very tired
My body runs on caffeine and good will
A little duct tape just here for lift

In my head is a very overwhelmed
Lonely for her Love woman
Running worries like numbers
123, 864 tabs running 24/7 365

I'd kill for a little rest and maybe
Some peace of heart,
A little psyche soother
A full night's rest with no nightmares

For now, I'll have more coffee and
Wait for it to be time to play
Human bean again

Melanie McCurdie

dangerous liaisons and cutthroat city

No, You don't. Believe me, as a prisoned resident, I know from personal experience that It's dangerous liaisons and cutthroat city in there. It's certainly no place for a tenderfoot such as yourself.

Huh. So you say, with that devilish grin and a flinty glint in those eyes and sure, I could crumble, but I won't. Not yet, maybe.

Come aboard, if you dare, should you care, and abandon your bravado at the door. I like it when my suitors scream ...

The Silent Way

I am indeed the best butt of some inside joke
snicker, sure, cos it seems legit to you to do it
but
Just think a minute - tick tock tick tick tick -
What if it were you? Huh, boo? What to do?
Easy to pretend, ignore, deny deny deny
But try to see it, look through my eyes
See how hard it can be?
To keep smiling while -
To keep fighting while -
To keep screaming while -
You are just a ghost disrupting
Someone's routine simply by existing
How hard it can be to be exposed to
Being treating as a mistreated dog
who shit on your lips life and
needs my nose rubbed constantly in it

Melanie McCurdie

bones don't lie

There's a woman in the mirror
that I barely recognize -
maybe a little around the eyes
and in the ghost of a smile
that seems to tremble on the verge
of - I'm not sure but I empathize
with the wistfulness that lies
behind the false facade window dressing
you know, maybe it's a blessing in disguise
that I don't know this
beautiful wretched creature
with the sad longing eyes
she's not what she used to be
the truth lays like bones
in the tears that threaten to spill
and I'd give anything to see them
overflow happy rather than hide
the misery away behind a
deep-seated desire to just fade away.

munday

She says her name is Munday,
blushing on the edge of shy,
With her amber highlights flushed,
she nearly glows in the ambiance.
Gently she lays in my hands
As though she were made for them,
and maybe she is.
How she is loved,
Monday quivers, breathlessly.
It sounds like scores of Seraphim
She quivers,
Just like a wounded bird when
I pluck at her heartstrings and
Listen to her sing so clear,
she sighs like the waves on the ocean and her voice,
I pluck her heartstrings again, and
together, how we tremble, anticipating.
Her voice is freedom's ring.
The sweetest sound in the world and she sings for me.

Melanie McCurdie

Shoe Print Angels

Youth's graceful ballet
Supple, kept alive,
so often, so quietly
It fades,
as prancing ponies do
It gets wiped away
by wrinkles and silver linings
And like footprints in the sand
We begin life again, older
These shrouded smiles
Some trapped in memories
Rather than photographs in albums
Are the faces of ghosts
Found in the shoe prints of angels
They are left behind to remind us that
Sometimes. Sadness may call
Like an unwanted late-night guest
If only to make us see that even
Snow is necessary to freeze us free
Lest we die with lessons forgotten

the accurate definition

I could climb the stairs
again and again
yes, I know that -
I do know that
its the accurate
definition of
insanity, but -
but what if it was
just as difficult
to stand in one place
staring at the door
for eternity
never knowing that
those stairs laying there
beyond the doorway
lead upwards and onwards
up to the stars as
well as downwards
to oblivion

it's a title wave

I feel so sad
it's a title wave -
a tsunami
and its becoming
more and more difficult
to hold back.

I'm not sure that
I want to any more,
hold back or
hold on
I'm not sure but
deep down inside
I just wonder why I'm here and
what purpose misery serves
in the grand scheme of things.

I wonder if it matters at all
and if it doesn't, why I bother.
If it does, then someone better give up the
fucking punchline because its exhausting to try
to smile when you are dying inside

a horrified shadow

*If you have never felt hunger
a desperation so deep in your gut
that it gnaws at your bones and
it speaks in vernacular tongues
whispering to your pain addled brain
in the devil's voice it denies,
tries to convince your starving stomach
that it doesn't need that sustenance
then you have no right to tell me to be patient.*

*It is devastating, to stand in the
refrigerator light sobbing,
in the open door of a food filled fridge and
know that there is not a damned thing in it
that you can ingest or imbibe
and there is nothing you can use
to fill that emptiness inside.*

*That experience
is enough
to destroy
anyone's
mental wellbeing*

Melanie McCurdie

hitting home

Just had to have it your way, ply and plead
over poetry and broken, useless promises
Pretty words meant to crack veneer,
like stones on a still frozen pond,
you just kept hammering it home
It did too, hit home, believe it.
a punch to the solar plexus
a knee to the box would've been kinder
I'm still standing, though bleeding out
still breathing, despite the arrows
You couldn't help yourself, again

I say it's bullshit, and a cop out.

lie to your heart, repeatedly;
do it so you can keep lying to mine.
by all means, keep spreading
lye on the few memories
that meant something to me
making me watch is cruel and all this
just makes it uglier and frankly,
I see enough horror in the mirror every day
Reality bites and it leaves scars behind
the kind that will never fade
A fact that'll hit home for you, too

the chesterfield

I used to overflow while sitting on a sofa -
Chesterfield - Couch, whatever.
Thighs spilled over edges, although not a lot,
and my gut filled my lap more than
the kids ever did

Today I sat in the same place, on different
furniture, in the corner and I barely filled
half of the cushion leaving nothing to spill over
And there was room on my lap for my bigger
baby boy and the mutt, although not a lot

Shortness of breath from walking was more
common than breathlessness for any other
reason. It's sad really.
Having no air is lovely
when it is stolen by beauty and is
much preferable to the fear of suffocating

Somehow, with my hands resting on my hips
I can feel the new points and jutting edges
the image that the mirror shows a stranger
I still don't feel like me

Melanie McCurdie

hEaD oN a StIcK

Sky eye blue tee
You see, because,
I feel less, well…alone in it
Bury my head in the pillow,
a last kiss goodnight
and hope to sleep before I cry

It rarely works

Pray, prey, for light
A direction from whatever
Omnipotent Entity chooses to answer

The Universe provides the proof
That I am not by myself
in yet another fight,

The same battle that
I don't want to fight anymore
I'm tired, I guess

If all else fails …at least tonight …
I can threaten people with my head on a stick

That might be fun
shrug

throwing stones

Let's throw stones, shall we?
No? You do already –
Don't be shy. Go ahead -

Now, as hard as you can
Throw it into the water
Watch the impact! Don't look away!

Smash the mirror image and
make the ripple reality
The splash is arterial spray or your own tears
And you killed it
Did it feel good? Did you enjoy it?

Do it again.
Do it again
Again!!

Beat that voice in your head into silence
Throw those stones like punches
Over and over til your arm hurts

Notice how the ripples destroy the reflection?
The cold clear sky reflects like
A slight mist on the surface of hell

It's too pretty

Throw more stones
Make it ugly
Make it *hurt*

Do it again
Again
AGAIN, DO IT AGAIN

Scream, Curse the sky
Throw rage to the river
Let it drown

Do Nothing
Let it die
cry

burden of truth

The burden of truth
Proof, whatever you call it
It's that temptation to burn
Scald your mind with scales

It's a weighted feather
A sip of gasoline dressed up as cognac
They tell you to drink it all down
One shot wonder, and you do

The world spins in your head,
Groans, bemoans that same old thing

Use your tenacity,
See, you don't want it bad enough
We give you all the veracity you need
You don't really need it
Just do as we do

Shut up. Fly straight
Accept the meal of lies
It's free, this rotted meal
Be grateful for what you get
For this meal you pay nothing
All you can swallow

Glut it up, but it'll cost you in the end
Once you are full you'll realise that
You can't handle the truth

Your proof is in perspective, and
After being force fed what you thought
Was a gourmet repast
You'll wish you could sick up

Such is the way we live, now
Sat before what appears to be
A legitimate spread
A peaceable feast
Is not more than another way
To indoctrinate your soul

Tricked Into accepting a lifetime membership
A place disguised as a country club
But is truly just a prison

snap

Edge of your seat folks!
More like edge of the bed
Live screaming
Live streaming tears
Talk about true horror
It's so loud
Too loud
Round and round
Only the hammers of hell drown
They fade out the noise

Stop beating yourself! but how?
How when your brain hates you
Dredging up some old fleshy skeletons
And they snap snap snap
They snap and snap and
It laughs while I squirm
While I scream and plead
Snap snap snap
Beat my own fists
Against the floor
Forehead against the bones
But it's all agony from there

Alone at 4:48 am and I can't breathe
Shiver and shake like a fever seizure

Melanie McCurdie

Listen to a voice suggesting solutions
But antidepressants are not the answer
They don't stop the nightmares;
The clawing for leverage
To keep myself from falling
The gasping for air to keep from drowning
The search for glue
to keep from falling to pieces
Or the quicksilver pain that follows on waking
dying in a drowning embrace

Passion burns, and she gasps
Earthshake quivering over a rigid rising
when he pulls the pleasure from her belly
Rhythmic motion of riding the ocean sighs
He watches desire rise from her chest
It's a tsunami of tangled bodies
Her cries rise like a bird in flight
Both clinging to love
like a life preserver
While dying in a drowning embrace

the back-burner yawp

You know,
All this magnificent mess before you,
Beauty by My Eyes Bloody Well Ache...
Remember me?
That brilliant bitch that resembles who I was?

It's tough on me too
It's hard on ME, too
Did you realise, that
I'm getting hit from all sides?
Forever explaining and justifying
Swallowing my hurt and lonely

Needy ass whiny bitch
Yeah yeah don't remind me
Emotions are a waste of time
Specifically when the only voice
That can be heard is the Poor Me Opus

Don't tell me to stop like it matters at all.
This how I punish myself
I beat myself for failing
Until I'm just tired of being tired
And sick of bleeding

Until I want that what's in that bottle

More then eating the self loathing
Maybe, I want to feel something burn
Other than my eyes

Yes. I know it's hard to remember
Things like, I'm a person.
I feel all this awkward weirdness
Lonely worthless bullshit, too

All of this is hard for me,
How bout a thought about that?
I hurt too.

I admit that I'm an asshole.
Again. And again. With my dying breath
If that would make you happy -
What more do you want me to do?

the noises above

I can hear the neighbors
Stomping like wild horses
Over my head and it's seems so simple
Just not a hard concept
But man apparently these people forgot
They live in apartments,
like the ones under their elephantine feet

Things are not rosy
They aren't fantastic and no
Please don't ask me to talk
It's a process and I'm not there yet
I'll babble when I'm ready, Freddy

Oh good. The baby wildebeest is back
Stomp stomp yell and scream
While I wait for the demon
that lives up above me
Winds his ass down and pass out

My mind drifts away on a star
In a car, it dreams while hit the throttle
Take over the wheel and hit the gas pedal
I'm stronger than this
Bitches better not try me
I don't want to complete,

Melanie McCurdie

I can't possibly win this battle
Hard as I try, I know that I won't

There are skirmishes I may win
But that's not the same
Things only look up when you put down the blame

I've been to these wars,
I don't want to relive them
If you cannot fight, I know I can't go it alone
The thunder has returned and .
I am drifting to dreamland
Not before I Holler goodnight
Then it is quiet

i know what overwhelmed feels like ...

It's personalised torture
straight from the brain
You can't breathe and
everything is too close

Then it's too hot – then cold – then hot
hands shake and bones creak
that twisting in the gut turns
along with your heart

You don't want to eat or drink
because you will be sick
nothing is appetizing you don't want to
You must, so you do and immediately regret it

that torture, it lies and says it will help,
it'll be okay, and it uses the voices of the
people you care about to tell you that
you can't do it

It doesn't help, and it isn't okay
it just makes everything worse, and
those other people don't matter
you know that too

So you stand there – you kneel, or you lay there
berating and grating, anticipation of explosions
more friendly fire, okay give up –
tomorrow is a new day

It's a new day, a new slay –
it is going to be both those things
You could go to sleep but will awaken
knowing that nothing has changed, and
that you've not one step further ahead

You're okay; it's all good, everything is fine,
no it's not, and there's that feeling of falling
where is the air? everything is too close again.

lawless mouth

I feel as though we live
in a world full of false faces
We are forced to wear masks,
act is life is hunky dory,
She wears a smile so all
is sunshine and daisies

It's a joke with no punchline.
Nobody wants to look
past their proboscis and
Past the mirror in their eyes

The hearts of mankind cry
It doesn't matter that
One's heart weeps from their eyes
Its easier to act and
Play pretend like children

Its okay,
There's nothing to see here
Just put on that smile, soldier
all are well adjusted here
And we smile and agree

Curiosity fails
No one asks what's under

The wrapping and trappings
No one acknowledges
the reality there

Pay no attention
to the woman behind
the gossamer curtains!!

Nobody deals with the
emotions that lay beneath
They just damn mask
Because they are told to
Wearing it frightens me.

Out of sight is out of mind
Minds, what's left after the
commonality cuts
we are all out of our heads and
Are encouraged to be

I'm playing the same game
I won't play the blame game
It's out of necessity
I wear it out of need
Out of sight isn't out of mind
It's a facade and I hate it

just. keep. breathing

Just keep breathing
I'm trying but I hate it
Wheezing, whining, crying alone
into a pillow in the dark

There are elephants on my chest and
they're giving gifts of huge butt wiggles
I wish they would leave now
its hard enough to breathe as it is

Still furiously, futilely fighting
the constant war battling between
the lines of belief and faith
The topic is always the same:
the views of what is right or always wrong

Gods damn it!
I know I'm right, for once,

I am so sick of it;
Always being viewed as less than intelligent
Because I am blonde.
Smarter than you, believe it

Melanie McCurdie

I know it, but just because I
Don't shove my smart down anyone's throat,
doesn't mean that you can make insults or
or tell me I'm wrong

not when the monster on my heart
is waking me dying [watching]
Trying to breathe through the cotton rag
someone shoved in my mouth
(The gagged can't scream)

While this elephantine weight of burden
twerks on my chest and I lay here waiting
Continuing to struggle
Just. Keep. Breathing.

watch the garden grow

I bury it deep
There, in the backyard by the smallish graves
of all of our pets - the poor things,
they're missed

•

I bury it and let it
Lay in the decay of pitiful corpses
In the lighter dark of the one ray of sunshine
That reaches that place

•

I bury it deep
Next to the bodies, where it is safe, warm
Where blood was spilled in sacrifice
The damp soil thirsts for more

•

The neighbourhood is silent
I sit in the yard, thinking and wondering
If it is just another dead seed
But maybe, with love,
with attention - and fertilizer,
I can watch it grow in the sun

•

Perhaps it will be a lovely small rose
It may not be perfect, hidden in the dark
I can already see the petals
bourgeoning life and opening slowly

Opening like a virgin's legs
Light, delight, breathe
Enticing it glows and
spreads its glistening folds

•

But maybe, with luck, I can watch it die too
Watch it darken, bleed raw at the edges,
Drooping and blackening with wilt
A flower, that seed, I returned to the Earth
Ashes to dashes
headpot or flowerpot

•

I buried it deep
There, in the backyard
But maybe, with love, with attention -
Hidden in the dark, maybe I can watch it grow
I can watch it die

One day -

•

it hasn't happened
Yet

too much

Too much.
You are too much.
You're a mother now;
you can't act that way.
Can't you tone it down?
Act your age please
Be an adult!

Gods woman,
You are just too much -
Too much of what?
Too much of a human who loves life?
Too real and raw for people to deal?
I'm too much emotion?
Too much rage?
Too much innocence
Shown for my age?
Too tall? too skinny?
Too blonde to have brain?
Too quiet and too loud?
How exactly am I too much?
The words leave marks
like bloodstains on my heart
And lights the fire of my temper
Allow me to address and refresh:

I. Am. Not. Too. Much.

If I am too much for you, darling,
Then trust me, you are not enough of anything
To be able to handle me
I AM too much of everything
that is very true
Too much for the weaker amongst us
To deal with, and that's a delight
Act my age?
I've never been this age before
Maybe I am
Maybe we aren't meant to count years
But collect experiences like Treasure
And I am not what I seem, not now
I am much, much more.
Before I was too fat to have worth...

"If you lost some weight
You would be so pretty," some said
"If you lost weight you'd be happier."

"If you lost weight you wouldn't be so lonely or feel alone."

But being alone isn't always being solitary
And happiness is not revolving around weight
It's lonely in a house full of people
With no one to talk to

And crying yourself to sleep where no one can hear

It's wandering though days wondering why
While contemplating your existence
And sometimes praying that when you sleep
You do not wake into the hell you must live in
Sometimes, it's a necessity
To be alone
But not when it's forced upon you
Because of somebody else's issues
No one should be lonely in a crowd
No one should suffer hating themselves
Because of other people's opinions
And no one should ever
be made to feel
that they are too much

it's a sleepless struggle

I'm tired, and I cannot do more than pace, the bed calls me, but all I'm able to do is walk in agony. My entire being is battle-sore from the war being fought in my heart.

Being awake and lonely, alone in a place I hardly recognise away from the one who knows me best sucks harder than put to words.

The pain makes me vulnerable, especially when time grows short and the world is so quiet that all I can hear is the screaming of my emotions. Then the screaming ends, and it really is too quiet and too dark.

I'd sell my soul to be able to rest. My brain yells at me to write down the terrible things Muse keeps showing me, but my fingers are stiff and atrophied and I'm too scared to close my eyes lest I lose the thread.

Sleepless – it feels like its been days, I remember the last. The night was short but full of love.

A Spark of Soul

Now I ache, and I lurk in the shadowy corners and in the not so sinister doorways, hoping for a break that hopefully doesn't include my mind or my limbs

bite me

You keep saying that I don't talk, nor do I express myself, well ask yourself why that could be. let's see you utilise that brain for more than sexual function or romantic fantasy – can you? ask yourself again why I don't scream from rooftops, from soul balconies what's locked inside of me. The way I love or hate, you'd investigate if it mattered at all, but it doesn't matter and hasn't for a while now.

the worst of it is that you continue to preach to disinterested passers by and still self serve a buffet of narcissistic platitudes that we are all expected to imbibe as gospel...not to mention the ballsy nerve to crown me drama queen because I break down and show my weaker side. Why you thought telling me that you can't decide what to say to me then running off to hide like a guilty child instead of the adult that you shout claim to be is beyond comprehension.

grow up already. I'm through with the raving, the whining, holier than thou, attitude when someone doesn't gift wrap your wants, your

needs, your deep desires, offered up ~~on~~ e
steaming on a stolen silver platter.

trust me, no one wants the half-gassed effort made at love so save the words and prove it for a fucking change instead of giving me a menu and the same shitty lip service that is always on tap

she knew

She knew something was wrong when he stopped bringing her flowers as a surprise, or coffee in bed or wanted an impromptu date to the grocery store with a milkshake after.

Those small things, like asking how she was, holding her hand, even a kiss goodnight ceased, and she noticed. She even used her words, spoke loudly; She stood *up* and told him how she was feeling. But nothing changed.

She knew something was really wrong when he stopped finding reasons to stay beside her in bed, instead of slipping quietly out. "I knew," she said to herself, when he stopped being interested in her body well after her brain. Or when he spent hours asleep on the sofa, or in bed, or got lost in a fog that stole his filter and ran away with his tongue.

She knew something was wrong when there was no conversation and little interaction, but to mention it became a lost cause. She knew when he'd be mean, and she'd cry because he promised that the tears wouldn't burn anymore, and they did.

She saw the signs, and knew, but as hard as she tried, she couldn't get through. She couldn't make him see that they were were dying and that words were just words.

Apologies are worth nothing more than the sounds they make after they've been offered in the same phrase time and time again.

Eventually, she gave up. They were carrying an empty shell; and somehow, he was sure no one could see that the love was dead until the stench of decay was too much to bear.

It's all over now but what she can't seem to live with is the wasted breath and the wasted years, all that time that she knew but stayed.

PONDERING

So its fairly late and I'm laying here in a dark room, petting the vocal Ms. Molly, and waiting for sleep to capture me. I have Hotel Transylvania 2 on the tube but sitting under the covers, all I can envision is Cinderella's evil stepmother Lady Tremaine, laying in her own bed, petting the less than angelic feline of her own, the endlessly lazy, Lucifer.

Granted, most cats are evil to some extent and although Molly is quite on the cuddly and solicitous end of the spectrum, the fact remains that she is still domesticus felis. Evil is in the genes. It's a fact, Jack.

With aching bones, I am left to wonder if Cindy's stepmom was really as awful as they portray or if perhaps Lady T, being of some advanced age, was just sore and tired. If maybe she was really just sick of the mice running amok about her home, of Lucifer's usual disinterest in anything remotely athletic such as chasing them out, and the constant bitching from those lazy brats of hers. I could understand her less than loving attitude if she lived with pain not only caused by teenagers.

Maybe, since Cindy didn't kvetch out loud and within earshot of the formidable Lady T about doing chores, and just helped out a lot by doing the work, she was simply overlooked and taken advantage of by an old woman tired of living in agony. Pain does make one tired, truly.

Maybe Lady Tremaine wasn't an evil stepmother but distracted, frustrated by her inability to traverse all those damned stairs, or go shopping with her friends, or run a marathon to the castle every summer. Maybe she was depressed by having to lay abed, taking comfort from Lucifer and waiting for the medication to take effect. Or tired from raising three kids on her own. I'm sure 3 girls of similar age bickering would take a lot out of anyone.

Maybe pain had made her mean instead of sweet, like it does me sometimes and she just had no other outlet but to lash out at whomever was handy.

These are the things I wonder about while I wait ...

loaded question

Why don't I believe in God? Well, that's a loaded question, my friend. I have my own reasons for disbelief in one man's God and reasons to believe as I do, and those are loud and clear to a precious few.

But since you asked, I'll offer you this:

I think the fundamental lessons that we learn from birth, like that unbidden and undefined trust in some omnipotent adult who sits watching while we are taught to pray for forgiveness is nothing but a lie.

To pray for sins that have yet to be committed, is less than logical to me. That we should kneel to beg or plead for saving, assistance, help, whatever you want to call it, also makes no sense to me.

This so-called God does little more than sit up there or down there, depending on your affiliation, watching those He claims to love to suffer and struggle as what, an object lesson?

Don't roll your eyes and sigh before I speak. Haven't we all listened to you and your projections of love and faith, and were you shakable? I know why I made my choice, do you?
You think because I don't practice faith as you do, that I know nothing but sweetheart, you know nothing about me.

I prayed. I was a faithful Daughter and I *prayed*, as I was taught to do. I prayed for strength and for help and for *someone*, anyone, to notice that I was dying inside.

When actual words didn't help, spoken to actual, physical people around me, I prayed, having lost my faith, I prayed for anything that would change the darker realities of life into light. I resorted to my childhood and I prayed to that God that I once believed would help me no matter what.

So why don't I believe? Because I learned a hard lesson when I was very young. I learned that ultimately trust is always going to be violated, and that that reality is much heavier than you can imagine; it'll crush you alive unless you learn to save yourself.

bite to the bone

... I changed?

And what exactly do you know about change?

This from someone who is still so tied to apron strings that you play frog to the command to jump every single time and from someone who has no right to ask you to do anything to boot.

Oh sure, make everyone and anyone else responsible, when you can offer nothing more than criticism, while sabotaging any situation to make yourself look better

I could never figure out how you could do that when you can't even look yourself in the mirror. What's more, when you get kicked in the face, get thrown to the wolves or under a bus ... you beg for more instead of using the backbone or the brain Goddess gave you

But I changed...

I begged you to make efforts; Asked for change for the sake of the many but all I ever got in return were the same bullshit excuses and platitudes laced with passive aggressive poison and tonne of empty promises

All I heard from your mouth were reasons why not, and rarely if ever did I hear the reasons why you could. Talk about throwing someone under the bus; I had more of my fair share there too...

But I changed....

I didn't know that word was in your vocabulary. In truth, I can hardly take the opinion into account of someone who plays the blame game so well that it has become the only truth you know.

To what end should I listen to the skewed thoughts from someone who has yet to accept their screws ups and own them, instead of deferring what you can't accept as fault

I guess it's easier to make me the bad guy than is to accept your own failures. It's easier to make someone else culpable, to place the weight anywhere but on your own shoulders.

But I changed...

Maybe I did. Maybe I did become healthier, at first, more confident until you tried to take that too. I own my part in the reasons why, but I will not own everything.

Perhaps, I didn't change but was less likely to listen to the constant assertions that I was wrong or accept the unacceptable any longer than I had. I wasn't the one lying while feeding monsters who ate money and spit out demands.

I waited for you to snap out of your delusions and wake the fuck up but that never happened. If it makes you able to sleep at night to believe that if I'm the one who made all the choices, so be it. At least I made the effort to save what mattered.

Can you claim the same?

ABOUT THE AUTHOR

Residing in Calgary, Alberta, you can most often find me writing horrific fiction, hanging out with my teen-aged kids, or shooting things with my camera in my free time. I am also a rabid supporter of Independent Film and Publications, and proudly a horror junkie with a taste for pretty things, words, and bloodsauce.

Made in the USA
Middletown, DE
01 June 2018